A Lobster's Tale

Written by

Michael P. Cifello

Illustrated by Denise Schroeck

In the memory of

my Gramma Dot

Dorothy Cifello

All rights reserved.

This book or parts thereof may not be reproduced

without the written permission of the author.

A Lobster's Tale Copyright 2001, Reprint 2009

mfn publishing PO Box 1156 Plymouth, Massachusetts

www.mfnpublishing.com   ISBN 978-0-9712519-1-5

American Printing, Rumford RI

My sincere appreciation for the support

and guidance of Charles A. Gates

*Special thanks to my wife Juliana,
Lynne Turner, Carol Gates and Ross Moore.*

A Lobster's Tale

Written by

Michael P. Cifello

Illustrated by Denise Schroeck

A Lobster's Tale

Macky Murphy was seven years old. He looked out at all the boats sailing through the Cape Cod Canal and wondered, "Where are they all going?" There were sailboats motoring by, powerboats skimming over the waves, and even a big merchant ship heading for Cape Cod Bay.

Macky was on vacation with his family. They planned to spend the summer on Cape Cod. His parents had rented a cottage for the week near the Cape Cod Canal. The family would then stay on the Cape for the remainder of the summer.

Macky had blonde hair and freckles on his nose. He and his dog Champ were the best of pals.

A Lobster's Tale

Macky and Champ walked along the canal road. The road begins at Scussett Beach, and meanders along the canal all the way to the train bridge in Buzzards Bay. All year long people walk, ride, rollerblade or just sit and enjoy the view, which is just what Macky and Champ were doing at that moment.

Macky's father called to them. It was time to go. They drove to the fish market located at the rotary that directs travelers from each direction to the Bourne Bridge.

A Lobster's Tale

The American Lobster Mart is shaped like a lighthouse. Inside all kinds of seafood is sold. On the walls are pictures of the Alice Marie, one of the lobster boats that catches the lobsters. They have a new lobster boat also, called the Virginia Marie. Bob and Denny handle the boats while their brother Tom manages the fish market.

Macky walked inside with his dad. The lobsters were kept in clear glass tanks. The water was kept very cold because they liked it that way. Most of the lobsters were just caught the day before and brought in on the Virginia Marie. As Macky's father talked to Larry the head cook, Macky inspected the tanks. They looked so big. Macky realized he was looking eye to eye at one of the biggest lobsters, and for a moment he thought it winked him.

A Lobster's Tale

Macky stepped back from the tanks, and then came closer for a better look.

He looked at the big lobster again and it seemed to be blowing bubbles at him. Larry started taking lobsters out of the tank and putting them into a box.

Macky's dad had ordered twelve lobsters. As Macky watched, Larry grabbed the big lobster that he had taken an interest in. When the big lobster came out of the water, Macky thought he heard a strange sound. Macky's dad carried the box of lobsters and put them in the back of the vehicle. He put a beach blanket over the box to keep the hot sun off the cool lobsters.

A Lobster's Tale

At the cottage, Macky's mom had just returned from the grocery store with all kinds of food for a big barbeque. His father brought the box of lobsters to the basement where a spare refrigerator was kept. The lobsters had been prepared so they could not hurt each other or anyone else. Thick elastics were placed around the claws so the lobsters couldn't grab on to each other or little boys fingers. But, Macky knew he had to be careful.

He opened the box and started putting the lobsters into the trays of the refrigerator. He needed two hands to lift the big lobster. All of a sudden, Macky heard a voice, "Don't do it." Champ barked at the box.

A Lobster's Tale

Macky looked into the box. Again the voice said, "Don't do it! Keep that fur ball away from me!" The big lobster's eyes stared at him. Again the voice said,

"Don't do it!"

"Don't do what?" asked Macky.

"Don't let that hairy thing eat me!" said the lobster.

Macky couldn't believe his eyes and ears. The lobster was now standing on top of the box and had lifted its claws as if it was in a boxing stance. "Champ won't eat you he hates fish!" said Macky.

"I'm not a fish," said the lobster, "I'm a Homarus Americanus. Louie is my name."

A Lobster's Tale

Louie tried to keep Macky from grabbing him but it was useless. Macky put Louie in the refrigerator, slammed the door and then ran outside. The cool refrigerator made the lobsters sleepy. Louie tried to open the door but it was too heavy for the crustacean.

Macky played with Champ for a while. Then they took a walk along the beach. Later that night, they watched the Plymouth fireworks. Macky thought the lights of all the boats in the bay looked like a big floating Christmas tree. After the fireworks Macky and Champ returned to the cottage for a needed night's rest. The ocean breezes made the sea buoys cling and clang.

Macky and Champ fell into a deep sleep.

A Lobster's Tale

In the middle of the night Macky heard a high pitched scraping sound. Champ began to moan because the high pitch sound hurt his ears. Macky got up and walked about the darkened house with Champ at his heels. The sound seemed to be coming from the basement. Together they slowly stepped down the basement stairs. The sound appeared to get louder and louder.

Macky reached over to the refrigerator, that held the lobsters captive. He opened the door. All the lobsters were wide-awake, scraping their claws against anything they could. Macky couldn't believe what he was seeing. He was stunned at the sight.

A Lobster's Tale

"What's the matter boy? Catfish got your tongue?" cried Louie. "If you are going to eat us, we might as well have a full belly. Got any fish heads?" he asked.

"My dad is going fishing in the morning. There is bait in the freezer." Macky replied.

"That figures! No fresh fish!" said Louie.

Macky said, "I'll thaw it out in warm water." Macky closed the door and went upstairs to the kitchen. Champ followed.

Just before the door closed, Louie put his big crushing claw in the way. "Ouch, that hurt!" yelled Louie. "Ok guys, help me push this door open. We are very close to freedom!" he cheered. All the lobsters converged backwards against the door, and eased the door open.

A Lobster's Tale

They all fell to the floor. Sounds of claws hitting the deck peppered the room. Quickly they scuttled about the room seeking refuge underneath anything they could find.

Minutes later, Macky and Champ returned with the thawed bait. Macky opened the refrigerator only to find the lobsters had seemed to vanish into thin air. Champ began to sniff about. He put his nose at the base of the couch. A moment later he yelped and ran outside. One of the lobsters had pinched Champ's nose.

Macky had an idea. He took the lobster crate and placed it on its side. Then he took the thawed squid and spread them inside the opening. He turned the lights off, and sat at the top of the basement stairs and waited.

A Lobster's Tale

Macky waited, waited and waited. Finally, he heard sounds of claws against the floor. He also heard Louie yell, "Its a trap!"

Macky turned on the light. He saw some lobsters in the crate. Other lobsters were on the floor trying to get to the bait. He quickly turned the crate over and began picking the other lobsters up off the floor. He counted eleven, one was missing. It was Louie.

Macky wanted Champ to help him but Champ was leery of the crustaceans. Macky warned Champ not to get too close to Louie. Champ now began to sniff the floor again. He walked over to a bookshelf and looked up. When Macky looked up, he saw Louie on the top shelf. This shelf kept a collection of rare seashells.

A Lobster's Tale

Macky knew that he wasn't supposed to play with them. They were made out of an expensive glass and very delicate. Louie held one shell in his claw. "Ok Sonny, its time to talk! You take us to the ocean or your mother is going to wonder how this shell got broken."

Macky yelled, "Don't do it! I'll do whatever you ask."

"That's better," said the hard shelled Louie. "Get some ice and put it in the crate to keep my buddies cool. You take us to the water and then I'll give you this crystal shell."

"Ok! Ok!" yelled Macky.

"Put the fur ball in your room and shut the door," added Louie.

A Lobster's Tale

Macky did as he was told, then returned. Louie was now on the floor next to the crate. Macky went over to the shelf and noticed some more shells were missing. "What's going on?" said Macky.

"Insurance that's all," said Louie. "Once we are in the water, I'll tell you where to find the rest of the shells. You can come back and put everything in place before your mother even wakes up."

Macky put Louie in the crate and carried it out the back door. It was very heavy. He closed the top and put the crate in his wagon. Then, he tied it to his bike. The lobster caravan headed for the beach. Louie pushed open the crate top to get a better look at his surroundings. He had to make sure Macky didn't try anything that might prevent his escape.

A Lobster's Tale

The sky began to get lighter. Macky pedaled the bike down the road. Soon the pavement turned to gravel and the ride became very bumpy. Louie was having a difficult time keeping the crystal seashell from moving about in his claw. " Take it easy kid. You don't want this thing to break do you?" said Louie Macky slowed down, and then brought the caravan to a stop.

He got off the bike, and untied the wagon. He pulled the wagon the rest of the way by hand.

The sun was just beginning to peek over Plymouth Bay. It was a wonderful sight. Fishing boats were heading out for their catch and a few people were walking on the beach. They were wondering what a boy was doing with a wagon full of lobsters.

A Lobster's Tale

The sand was getting deeper and it was becoming harder and harder to pull the wagon. All of a sudden he heard a horn beep. It was his father in the parking lot. Macky was almost to the water when he heard his father yell to him. "Macky, what are you doing?"

Macky didn't stop. Macky started to toss the lobsters into the water.

Lastly, he looked at Louie and said, "Ok, hand it over."

"Put me in the water first," said Louie. Macky put him gently in the water.

His father was almost to them. Louie let go of the crystal shell and said "Look under the couch for the others. See ya later kid" said Louie. And just like that, he was gone.

A Lobster's Tale

His father was breathing very hard as he approached Macky. "Why did you let the lobster's free son?" asked his father.

Holding the crystal seashell, Macky replied, "Dad it's a long story. Can we talk about it over breakfast?"

"Breakfast Macky!" his mother called. "Time to wake up for breakfast!" she said again.

Macky looked up at the ceiling and then out the window. He jumped out of his bed and ran to the basement. He went over to the refrigerator and looked inside. It was empty.

He laughed to himself, " It was all a dream." Then he said to Champ, "Everyone knows lobsters can't talk." Champ agreed. Both Champ and Macky had their breakfast.

A Lobster's Tale

After breakfast, Macky got dressed and went to the Cape Cod Canal. It was a beautiful day. He noticed a seagull had landed on a nearby rock. Macky felt that this was going to be a great vacation. He skipped some stones on the water, and Champ barked at the seagull.

THE END

Please take a moment and visit our website at www.whereslouie.com

Or at www.mfnpublishing.com

A Lobster's Tale

Coming Soon…another book by Michael P. Cifello

"OFF SEASON"

The Adventure's of a seagull named,
Charles C. Gull